THE ROAD TO 180

THE ULTIMATE GUIDE TO LSAT PREP

COMPREHENSIVE LSAT PREP
ON MOBILE & WEB

lsatmax.io/180

Claim Your Free 30-Min LSAT Consultation

Ensure a strong start to your LSAT prep. Schedule your free LSAT consultation with a *99th percentile instructor*.

Visit lsatmax.io/consultation or Call (855) 294-4553

Try The #1-Rated LSAT Prep for Free.

- ⚡ **Instant & Lifetime Access**
- 📄 **90 Full Length LSATs**
- % **99th Percentile Instructors**
- 📱 **Authentic Digital LSAT/ LSAT-Flex Experience**

- 📈 **Detailed Analytics**
- 🕐 **Weekly Office Hours**
- 🎖 **Higher Score Guarantee**
- 🏅 **#1 for 3 Years in a Row**

Get 10% Off When You Enroll.

Kyle Ryman
Texas A&M

I scored below a 150 on my first practice LSAT in November. **In June I took the LSAT and scored a 170. I couldn't have done it without LSATMax.**

Anita Yandle
University of Washington

The tutorials from LSATMax helped me get my 99th percentile score! It was great to have the videos at my fingertips at all times so that I could study any time I had a moment.

Austin Sheehy
University of Central Oklahoma

LSATMax is my hero! **My starting score was around a 155-158, and I scored a 170 on the June LSAT!**

Naader Banki
USC

I used LSATMax to study for the October LSAT. **I started out with a diagnostic somewhere in the 150s, and improved my score to 166 on the October test.**

To Redeem Visit lsatmax.io/180 or Call (855) 294-4553

Want a high level of personalized attention from the best of the best?

Get Live 1:1 Attention from **99th Percentile Tutors.**

Visit **lsatmax.io/tutoring**

Want to gain insights about law school admissions and the LSAT?

Subscribe to Our
Insider Content Series
with Mehran.

Instagram Live
Sessions

@lsatmax

The Legal Level
Podcast

on iTunes

Visit lsatmax.io/insider

LONG IS THE WAY, AND HARD, THAT OUT OF HELL LEADS UP TO LIGHT.

John Milton

TABLE OF CONTENTS

QUESTIONS YOU SHOULD ASK

INTRODUCTION

Congratulations! You have taken the first step in deciding to go to law school. Whether you are just starting to prep for the LSAT or you are trying to maximize your LSAT score, we understand your struggle. We've been there!

LSATMax was created because our founder, Mehran Ebadolahi, realized while studying for the LSAT that traditional in-class LSAT courses did not provide the tools he needed to maximize his score. When Mehran's in-class course ended and his access to the course materials was discontinued, he was nowhere near his target score so he decided to postpone his exam date and self-study for a few more months. He eventually raised his score by 26 points, scoring a 174 on the December 2004 LSAT, and gained admission to Harvard Law School.

During his time at Harvard, he decided to fix the problems he saw in test prep. After creating BarMax, one of the top bar exam review courses available, he moved on to create LSATMax, the first comprehensive LSAT course available in the App Store. LSATMax was created to give all students access to high-quality LSAT prep at an affordable price. We feel that everyone should have the opportunity to get the highest possible score on the LSAT, particularly since the LSAT is by far the number one factor in law school admissions.

When Mehran first decided to pursue law school and take the LSAT, he was completely lost. In fact, he walked out of his first practice LSAT seriously reconsidering his law school dream. He had many questions and needed guidance, but had no single, dedicated place to turn for answers.

Enter this book. In order to combat the daunting and confusing task of beginning (or continuing) your LSAT prep, we have created a list of the top ten frequently asked LSAT questions (i.e., Commonly Asked Questions) and the top ten "should-ask" LSAT questions (i.e., Questions You Should Ask). In this book, we provide the answers to those questions.

Take a deep breath. We've got your back.

The road to 180 starts here.

COMMONLY ASKED QUESTIONS

What Is The LSAT?

The Law School Admission Test (LSAT) is a half-day standardized test that is administered multiple times each year at designated testing centers throughout the world. The test is an integral part of the law school admission process in the United States, Canada, and a growing number of other countries, making up 75-80% of the admissions decision. It provides a standard measure of acquired reading and reasoning skills that law schools use as the main factor in comparing applicants.

LSAT Format Overview

The LSAT consists of five 35-minute sections of multiple-choice questions, four of which contribute to your score. The unscored section, commonly referred to as the experimental section, is used to pretest new LSAT questions. The placement of this section will now vary because, as of October 2011, LSAC removed the previous rule that required the experimental section to appear in the first three sections (i.e., before the break). A 35-minute writing sample used to be administered at the end of the fifth section but, as of June 2019, you will now complete the writing sample online at a time and place of your choosing. You will be able to take LSAT Writing on the day of your LSAT administration and for up to one year thereafter. LSAC does not score the writing sample, but a copy of the writing sample will be sent to all law schools to which you apply.

Historically, the LSAT has been a paper-and-pencil test. This is still the case for international LSATs, at least for the time being. In the United States and Canada, however, the LSAT is now a digital exam administered on a Microsoft Surface Go tablet.

Tablets will be provided to test takers at the test center. On the digital LSAT, both the content and the structure of the test sections and the questions will be the same as the paper-and-pencil LSAT. But in addition, the digital LSAT will include new features such as a timer with a five-minute warning, highlighting, underlining and flagging to keep track of questions that you may want to revisit in a section.

While this is undoubtedly the biggest in change in history of the LSAT, tablet-based digital LSATs are nothing new for **LSATMax**. We have been offering full-length, officially licensed LSATs on both iPads and Android tablets since 2012, so you can rest assured that our 5-star rated app will allow you to simulate the new digital LSAT experience on every official Prep Test.

lsatmax

Available in the App Stores
and lsatmax.io/180

In addition to the LSATMax app, you can also simulate the digital LSAT experience on iPads and Android tablets using our newest app, **Practice LSATs** by LSATMax.

Practice LSATs

Available in These App Stores

Logic Games

Every Logic Games (aka Analytic Reasoning) section consists of 22-25 questions with 4 different games, each containing anywhere from 5 to 8 questions. These questions measure your ability to understand a structure of relationships and then draw logical conclusions about that structure. You are asked to reason deductively, using a set of statements and rules that describe relationships among people, things, or events.

Analytical Reasoning questions reflect the kinds of complex analyses that a law student performs in the course of legal problem-solving. As with all other types of questions on the LSAT, there is a finite number of "types" of questions. All Logic Game questions will have some type of inventory, whether it's people, canoes, apples, or wombats. You are then asked to place the inventory in some type of order: sequential, grouped, or just based upon the sometimes-convoluted conditions that the LSAC will give you. Really, Logic Games are no different than a Sudoku puzzle, and the great thing about the games is that they are actually easier than Sudoku. After you have seen a few hundred questions, they will become familiar—even predictable. One very important thing to remember about the LSAT is that it is repetitive.

Your goal is to come up with a system to draw out a setup and symbols that depict the rules you're given. It is essential to develop a setup and rule diagrams that correctly reflect the conditions; in turn, this will allow you to move through each question accurately and efficiently. Once you have your rules written down, you will want to plug them back into your setup.

For example, a Logic Games question could present the following scenario: six bloggers—Jake, Karla, Laith, Melody, Neema, and Olivia—are standing in line, one in front of the other, to purchase tickets to see the *Avengers: Endgame*. The conditions could be as follows: 1) Jake is in front of Melody, 2) Karla is in front of Olivia, 3) Jake is not in front of Neema, and so forth.

In creating your rule diagrams, you would depict condition #1 like this: J > M. The great thing about the games is that you can use whatever symbols you want, and arrange them the way you like best—so long as you are CONSISTENT! Let's try condition #2: K > O. Now let's go for #3: your first instinct may be to write "not J > N." However, it is always best to write out your symbols, if possible, in the positive. So, let's think. If all six bloggers are in line, and Jake is NOT in front of Neema, then Neema is in front of Jake, right? Right! So we would write it out as such: N > J. Bravo!

Logical Reasoning

While there is only one scored Logic Games section and one scored Reading Comprehension section on the LSAT, there are two scored Logical Reasoning sections. Therefore, 50% of your score is Logical Reasoning.

Each section has anywhere from 24 to 26 questions. These questions assess your ability to analyze, critically evaluate, and complete arguments as they occur in ordinary language. Each Logical Reasoning question requires you to read and comprehend a short passage (aka the stimulus), then answer a question about it. The questions are designed to assess a wide range of skills involved in critical thinking, with emphasis on the skills central to legal reasoning. These include the ability to draw well-supported conclusions, the ability to reason by analogy, and the ability to determine how additional evidence affects an argument, all while applying defined principles or rules and identifying logical fallacies.

Most stimuli presented in this section are arguments, which consist of two main parts: the premises (i.e., the evidence or support) and the conclusion. Usually, some scientist or spokesperson is drawing a ridiculous conclusion based upon evidence that is not necessarily connected to (or supportive of) that specific conclusion.

You might see, for instance, something like, "Naz likes only delicious foods. All red apples are delicious. Therefore, Naz likes red apples." Here, the speaker has arrived at the incorrect conclusion that just because Naz **only** likes delicious foods, and red apples are delicious, Naz **must** like red apples. What assumption has the speaker made? The speaker has assumed that Naz likes all delicious foods, which must then include red apples. In fact, however, a food must be delicious for Naz to like it, but just because it is delicious does not necessarily mean she will like it. To put this in terms you will soon be very familiar with, the delicious quality of a food is necessary, but not sufficient, for Naz to like it.

A very important thing to keep in mind while in this section (and, for that matter, in all LSAT sections) is that the words you see in the stimulus are your world. If, for instance, the stimulus says, "William Shakespeare wrote *Death of a Salesman*," then no matter how egregious the error, you must take it at face value and begrudgingly move forward. The words in the question are your world, and you know nothing beyond that stimulus for the purposes of this exam.

Now, back to our "red apple" example. The speaker has incorrectly assumed that just because Naz likes only delicious foods, she has to like all delicious foods. But, according to the evidence presented in the stimulus, this is not necessarily true. The premise—Naz likes only delicious foods—actually leaves open the possibility that Naz could dislike certain delicious foods, including red apples; this possibility destroys the validity of the conclusion.

Here is another important thing to remember: although you should never question the evidence that is given to you, you must *always* question the link between that evidence and the conclusion. For example, let's look at the following stimulus: "Recent studies have shown that some male giraffes have blue tongues. Therefore, some female giraffes must also have blue tongues." You should not question the evidence (i.e., that recent studies of male giraffes have taken place). Accept as fact that recent studies have shown that there are some male giraffes with blue-colored tongues. But you absolutely must question the conclusion by asking what evidence about male giraffes has to do with *female* giraffes.

Remember, the LSAT is very repetitive. There are about 16 variations of question types on the Logical Reasoning portion. Learn the specific skill and technique for each question type; then, all you have to do is identify the question type and apply the respective technique to find the correct answer. Practice is key.

Reading Comprehension

Each Reading Comprehension section consists of 4 passages, each of roughly 400-500 words. You will receive 3 solitary passages and 1 comparative passage. Each passage is followed by 5 to 8 questions for a total of 25-28 questions. These questions measure your ability to read and comprehend examples of lengthy and complex materials similar to those you will commonly encounter in law school.

There is always one passage on the arts or literature (the humanities), one passage on the natural sciences, one passage on the social sciences, and one passage on a topic related to law. You will be asked to identify the author's main point, tone, and purpose. You will have to make inferences based upon the information you have read, and pinpoint specific information found in the passage.

The first hurdle you must face is understanding that it is not the questions that are stumping you—it is that you may not be used to reading annoyingly dense articles very quickly, and actually absorbing the information presented (particularly when you have zero interest in the subject-matter!).

It is all about the **main point**, **the tone**, and the **purpose**. After you read each passage, stop for a second and answer these three questions:

(1) What was the passage about?

(2) How was the information conveyed to the reader?

(3) Why was the information conveyed to the reader? (e.g., to right a misconception, to inform, to persuade, etc.)

The answers to these three questions will help you tame the Reading Comprehension section. Get used to knowing the what, how, and why of each passage. You will soon see how great an asset this information can be. The not-so-secret secret about the Reading Comprehension section is that almost every question is a Must Be True question. This means that every correct answer is based on a corresponding line (or lines) in the passage. Practice finding these "liners" for each question, and soon you will see that the correct answers are right in front of you!

Writing Section

The very last section of the LSAT is the Writing Section, which is ungraded.

The writing section will now be separate from the LSAT and administered on a secure online platform. This change will result in greater convenience and flexibility for you as the testing day will be shorter, the essay will be typed rather than handwritten, and it can be completed at a time and place of your choosing. Students who sit for an official LSAT will be automatically eligible to complete the writing section as of the date of the LSAT and up to one year thereafter. You are only required to have one essay on file to complete your Law School Reports. Essays completed during previous LSAT administrations will still be valid for use in Law School Reports.

The Writing Section includes a prompt that describes a situation in which you need to make a decision. The prompt is never something controversial, so it will be an easy decision. There will be two options, and each one has pros and cons. There is no right answer. For example, you might get something like this:

> *BLZ Stores, an established men's clothing retailer with a chain of stores in a major metropolitan area, is selecting a plan for expansion. Using the facts below, write an essay in which you argue for one of the following plans over the other, based on the following two criteria:*
>
> *The company wants to increase its profits.*
>
> *The company wants to ensure its long-term financial*

stability.

The "national plan" is to open a large number of men's clothing stores throughout the country over a short period of time. In doing this, the company would incur considerable debt. It would also have to greatly increase staff and develop national marketing and distribution capabilities. Many regional companies that adopted this strategy increased their profits dramatically. A greater number tried and failed, suffering severe financial consequences. BLZ is not well known outside its home area. Research indicates that the BLZ name is viewed positively by those who know it. National clothing chains can offer lower prices because of their greater buying power. BLZ currently faces increasingly heavy competition in its home region from such chains.

The "regional plan" is to increase the number and size of stores in the company's home region and upgrade their facilities, product quality, and service. This could be achieved, for the most part, with existing cash reserves. These upgrades would generally increase the prices that BLZ charges. In one trial store in which such changes were implemented, sales and profits have increased. The local population is growing. BLZ enjoys strong customer loyalty. Regional *expansion could be accomplished primarily using BLZ's experienced and loyal staff, and would allow continued reliance on known and trusted suppliers, contractors, and other business connections.*

Again: there is no correct answer, so all you have to do is choose the option that tickles your fancy the most; then, argue for the option you chose and against the option you did not. This is not the time to be creative or think outside of the box. That means you should not choose both options, or make up a third option.

Do not stress out about this section. Just complete it to the best of your ability, and hopefully, you will be done with the LSAT forever. During your LSAT prep, we recommend glancing at a Writing Section prompt once or twice, but there is no need to try your hand at "taking" a Writing Section. For many students, the first time they ever see a Writing Section is on their actual LSAT. A lot of law school admissions boards disregard the writing sample. Of the 157 schools that LSAC surveyed, 25.3% reported that they seldom used the writing sample in their decision, and 32.7% responded that they only occasionally used the writing sample.

How, exactly, should you write it? Well, remember that rote, five-paragraph, argumentative essay structure you learned way back in middle school? There was an introductory paragraph, followed by three analytical paragraphs, and it ended with a concluding paragraph. Ring a bell? Use that. Make sure to praise your option and, in doing so, show the weaknesses of the option you did not choose. Write it well, using complete sentences. Do not use words you do not fully understand or cannot spell, and make sure to keep it simple and to-the-point.

What the LSAT Measures

Here's the official answer: the LSAT is designed to measure skills considered essential to success in law school. These include the ability to read and comprehend a series of complex texts with accuracy and insight; the ability to organize, manage and draw reasonable inferences from information; the ability to think critically; and the ability to analyze and evaluate other people's reasoning and arguments.

Here's our answer: the LSAT tests a way of thinking. Point blank. Unlike other standardized tests, the LSAT is not testing your ability to memorize and regurgitate specific subject matter. Most students are not used to thinking in the way that formal logic and the LSAT demand. Preparing for the LSAT is all about getting yourself to master this form of thinking and problem-solving.

Repeating the LSAT

As of September 2019, however, you are permitted to take the LSAT 3 times in a single year, 5 times within the current and past five testing years and a total of 7 times over a lifetime. This new retake policy is forward-looking, not retroactive, so LSATs taken prior to September 2019 will not count against these numerical limits.

LSAC rules aside, however, sitting for an LSAT exam takes energy, time and money, so you should try to be fully prepared before attempting to take the exam.

Also, different law schools have different approaches to multiple LSAT scores. The good news is that most law schools no longer average LSAT scores (if you have taken the exam two or more times). Some do, however. Thus, you must research whether the law schools you are interested in do or do not average multiple test scores. If a law school in which you are interested does average scores, and you don't think you've performed as well as you could have, you will want to cancel if it's not too late. Otherwise, on your second sitting for the LSAT, you'll have to aim for an LSAT score high enough to balance out your first score (i.e., to get you into the 25th—75th percentile for the school you want to attend).

The rule of thumb here is to make sure you are ready before you take the exam. There is nothing wrong with postponing your exam date.

Sometimes, extenuating circumstances come into play. You may walk into your testing center completely ready, but walk out feeling less than happy. If you believe the LSAT score you received does not reflect your true ability—for example, if circumstances such as illness or anxiety prevented you from performing as well as you might have expected—you should cancel your score, and take the exam again.

When Can I Take the LSAT?

Unlike other graduate school entrance exams, such as the GMAT or GRE, the LSAT is not offered year-round. Until recently, the LSAT was administered only four times each year. Between June 2019 and April 2020, however, the exam will be administered nine times (June 2019, July 2019, September 2019, October 2019, November 2019, January 2020, February 2020, March 2020, and April 2020).

Only three of these tests will be "disclosed," meaning that LSAC will release the scored sections so you can review the questions. Disclosed exam administrations between

June 2019 and April 2020 are: (1) June 2019, (2) September 2019, and (3) November 2019. The remaining exams are nondisclosed.

It is important to decide which specific LSAT you would like to take, so you can plan out your study schedule.

Three of the nine LSATs to be administered in 2019-20 will take place on Saturday morning, starting at 8:30 a.m. local time (September 21, 2019; February 22, 2020; and April 25, 2020). For Sabbath observers, Saturday LSATs are also administered on the following Monday. You must submit additional documentation to LSAC before being allowed to take a Saturday LSAT on an alternative date.

The remaining six LSATs will take place on Monday, starting at 12:30 p.m. local time (June 3, 2019; July 15, 2019; October 28, 2019; November 25, 2018; January 13, 2020; and March 30, 2020).

Most law schools require that you take the LSAT by December at the latest for admission the following fall. However, taking the test earlier is often advised. Think about it: if you give yourself more time between the last possible LSAT you can take and your first LSAT, then just in case you feel unprepared or receive a score you are not positively ecstatic about, you have the chance to re-take the exam.

The main thing to remember is that almost every law school has rolling admissions. This means that the first application in is the first application read. The longer you wait, the later your application will appear in the queue—which can decrease your chances of admission. Ideally, you want your application to be seen by an admissions officer as early as possible, so you are being compared to fewer applicants while competing for a greater number of available seats.

However, if you are choosing between applying earlier with a lower LSAT score and applying later with a higher LSAT score, always choose the latter.

What is a Good LSAT Score?

Let's put things into perspective. The average LSAT score is 151. If you are scoring above that, then you are above average. However, if your sights are set on a Top 20 law school, then a score of 151 will not cut it.

A common misconception in the world of the LSAT revolves around what, exactly, constitutes a "good score." You will hear some people say that the minimum is 170. Others will say anything above a 165; still others may even say anything above a 155. Where is this discrepancy coming from? A "good" LSAT score is subjective, because it is based upon where you want to go to law school. A

167 could be a good LSAT score for one person, while a 154 could be a good LSAT score for another.

So, to figure out what a "good" LSAT score is for your own purposes, you must first figure out where you want to go to law school. Then, you need to determine the LSAT score range necessary for you to have a realistic chance of gaining admission to your school of choice. Many law schools publish "entering class profiles," which give applicants a sense of successful applicants' LSAT score ranges and GPAs. For example, a law school may have a 25th percentile score of 157 and a 75th percentile score of 162, which means that 25 percent of the admitted students score at or below a 157, 50 percent score between a 157 and a 162, and 25 percent score at or above a 162. To maximize your chance of acceptance into this school, you should NOT take the LSAT until you are consistently scoring well within this 157-162 range on your practice LSATs. Ideally, you want to score above a 162 (i.e., the 75th percentile).

Remember, your LSAT score makes up 75-80% of your application!

If you would like more information about different law schools and their admissions requirements, download our free iOS app, **Law School Match**.

Law School Match

Available in the App Store

What is the Best Way to Prepare for the LSAT?

The way you should prepare for the LSAT can be broken down into two simple steps: (1) understand and (2) practice.

The first step is to understand the concepts and strategies associated with each and every question type on the LSAT. How does one do this? Later in this guide, we will delve into the benefits of taking an LSAT prep course and, further, what type of LSAT prep course is best. Ultimately, through the materials you use, the hope is that you will create a cache of proven strategies and techniques that you can apply to each question type on the LSAT.

Once you have become acquainted with these strategies, the next step is to practice them—a lot. Remember, the LSAT is testing a way of thinking. Therefore, the only way you can truly get a strong grasp on it is to put in a lot of time and practice. Stated another way, dedicated practice is the second step. You should practice with as many real LSAT questions as possible, but remember, it is not just about taking as many practice LSATs as you can.

Rather, the key to your success is ANALYZING your work when you practice. When you have finished a practice section or exam, take a quick break; then, while the questions are still fresh in your mind, go back to the beginning of the section or the exam and go over all the questions again—this time without any time pressure. Make sure to go through all of the questions, especially those you were hesitant about. Reviewing the questions before you grade the section or the exam forces you to review it in its entirety, as opposed to only those questions you got wrong. During this review process, you can realize what you misunderstood when you took the section or exam under time pressure, and you should change your answers accordingly (but make sure to note what you originally selected).

Once you have gone over each question again, grade the practice section or exam as it was before you re-took it without time pressure (i.e., before you changed any of your selections). Review any questions that are still incorrect, as well as any questions you changed during your initial review.

We'll get into the importance of using real, officially-licensed LSAT questions later, but for now, know that the idea behind this fundamental tenet of standardized testing is to mirror the exam as closely as possible. Additionally, with 87 real, officially-licensed LSATs currently available and 3 more being released in 2019, there is no way you will run out of real questions to practice with. Again, LSAC releases a list of the LSAT prep providers using real, officially licensed questions, so make sure any course you are considering appear on this list.

The LSAT is like a marathon. When you decide to run a marathon, you do not start preparing with an all-out, 26.2-mile sprint. You take it slowly, step by step. You work your way up to the actual event. Once you are able to run the full 26.2 miles, you will want to run the course of the marathon prior to the actual race, so you can get yourself acquainted with the obstacles coming your way. You must train in a similar way for the LSAT. If your test is in the morning, you need to get your mind accustomed to being fully alert at 8:00 a.m., and ready for four hours of intense concentration. You want to be as exact as possible; so if your exam is on a Saturday, take your full-length practice LSATs on Saturday mornings. Make your mind equate Saturday mornings (or whenever your exam date and time is) with logic and concentration.

Another big thing to remember is that the LSAT has no penalty for wrong answers. This means that there should never be ANY unanswered questions on your exam. Even if you are running out of time, be sure you leave time to select answers for any questions you may not have answered. If you are guessing, just choose a letter, and always select the same letter.

Should I Take an LSAT Prep Course?

The value of an LSAT prep course is learning the concepts and strategies associated with the different exam sections and question types.

Though an LSAT prep course is neither necessary nor sufficient for getting the score you want, it is highly recommended. While some people self-study for the exam and score in the 170s, most do not have the correct materials, self-discipline, organization, or stamina required to successfully self-study for the LSAT.

For most people, the way of thinking tested on the LSAT

is novel. For this reason, it is advisable to take an LSAT prep course to get you acquainted with the exam, and what techniques and strategies to use. You, however, need to make this decision for yourself.

Let's go through some pros and cons of taking an LSAT prep course:

PRO: For those of you who have a harder time motivating yourself to study, a course offers more structure through a set schedule of assignments to complete. This puts less pressure on you to create and complete a study schedule/syllabus for yourself.

CON: Depending on the course you choose, this can actually be a huge waste of your precious prep time. Many courses are not only inefficient in the schedules they create for you, but also use materials other than officially-licensed LSAT questions, which means you end up spending a lot of time studying materials that may never appear on the exam. Thankfully, LSAC now publishes a list of official licensees so you should definitely confirm that the course you are considering appears on this list (LSATMax does!; TestMax, Inc. is the name of our company).

PRO: Your LSAT prep course will make sure you are armed with tons of materials. This way, you will not have to spend your time searching high and low for prep materials.

CON: The materials mentioned in the above "pro" might not actually be helpful. If you don't choose a course carefully, you could be taught incorrect strategies and/ or handed thousands of made-up LSAT questions that are not representative of actual LSAT questions.

PRO: Your prep course could (and should) help you learn proven techniques and strategies for each and every LSAT question type. Instead of trying to figure out how to approach each question type on your own, you will have the benefit of a quality course that will hand this information to you. With this foundation in place, you can continue your LSAT prep by practicing and honing the strategies and concepts you've learned on real previous LSATs.

CON: The quality of instruction in LSAT prep courses varies greatly due to the high turnover rate of LSAT prep instructors, and the fact that many companies do not even require their instructors to have scored in the 99th percentile on an actual LSAT. Some companies only require a 160 while others do not require their instructors to have even taken an official LSAT.

PRO: The LSAT is unlike any exam you have ever taken.

Taking an LSAT prep course will, if anything, help you become accustomed to formal logic and critical thought.

CON: Almost every LSAT prep course on the market *except* LSATMax will limit your access to course prep materials to 10 to 12 weeks, and charge you again if you want continued access thereafter. Since the LSAT is testing a way of thinking, however, the vast majority of students are not fully prepared within 10 to 12 weeks, so losing access to these course materials is less than ideal.

Remember, these are just a few things to consider. Taking an LSAT prep course, no matter which one you choose, is not absolutely necessary to obtaining your target score, but it is highly recommended.

If you do decide to take an LSAT prep course, make sure to select one that also gives you access to as many real, officially-licensed LSAT questions as possible.

Are There Any Classes in Undergrad That Will Help Me with the LSAT?

Many people recommend taking a few formal logic courses during undergrad. Though this may seem to make some initial sense, it is actually a big waste of your time—not to mention a great way to potentially lower your precious GPA.

Remember, the LSAT does not test content learned in school. It tests a way of thinking. Though taking classes in logic, philosophy, or critical reading and/or writing can prepare you for the mindset of analyzing complicated theories or texts, taking an entire semester to learn these techniques (at the risk of bringing down your GPA) is unnecessary, and a waste of time. Logic courses are far more in-depth than what you need to know for purposes of the LSAT.

These courses will not teach you the strategies you need for the LSAT, so unless they are already required for your major or minor, it's more conducive to focus your prep on materials actually tested on the LSAT.

How do I Improve My Timing?

When you begin to prepare for the LSAT, timing should not be your primary concern. No one will care that you were able to finish each section on time if you get all of the questions wrong. As you hone your techniques and strategies, you will see that your timing will soon catch up.

Another thing to keep in mind is that your LSAT timing goal, just like your LSAT target score, is subjective. If your goal is to score in the 170s, you will eventually need to get yourself to the point of having enough time to read, understand, and answer every question. However, if your goal is to score in the 160s, you do not need to get to every question. We have seen many students aiming for a 160 rush to finish exam sections; in doing so, they sacrificed accuracy for quantity of bubbles filled in, ironically lowering their scores.

In each section of the LSAT, there are easy, medium, and difficult questions. You gain the same amount of points for getting an easy or medium question correct as you do for getting a difficult question correct. Therefore, instead of sacrificing your accuracy on the easy and medium LSAT questions just to get to the difficult ones—which you might end up missing anyway—why not (at least until you are at a point where you feel you have no timing issues and are very comfortable with your accuracy) just slow down and make sure you get all the easy and medium LSAT questions correct? Worry about getting the questions correct *before* you worry about getting them correct under time pressure. Pace yourself. Your timing will improve with practice, not force.

Another thing to keep in mind is that as you begin to learn new strategies, you will actually slow down a great deal. This is because you are now trying to implement a strategy, as opposed to just reading the question and trying to answer it. However, as you continue to implement these strategies, your comfort with them will improve, as will your timing. Diagramming sufficient and necessary conditions is a perfect example of this.

As we have explained, there are a total of 5 sections on the LSAT. You have all of three and a half hours to finish them. The breakdown is 35 minutes per section. We believe it is most helpful to get a general mastery of each section and question type down before you really start worrying about timing. Again, it REALLY doesn't matter if you finish the section on time if you are not doing it accurately.

When you are ready to think about timing, your end-goal should be to finish each Logic Game and each Reading Comprehension passage in 8 minutes and 45 seconds, and each Logical Reasoning question in 1 minute and 24 seconds, on average. Remember, some questions may take less time than the average. Factor that extra time into questions that may be a little harder for you.

Remember, the digital LSAT includes a timer in the top right hand corner of the screen so you no longer have to worry about bringing your own analog timer to your testing center. This digital timer counts down from 35 minutes and you will receive a pop-up warning when there are 5 minutes remaining in the section.

How Long Should I Study for the LSAT?

Ideally, preparing for the LSAT should be your part-time job (i.e., four to six hours per day). Your baseline is to follow the calendar your LSAT prep course has provided for you. As for total time, you should ideally set aside around four to six months to prepare for the LSAT. You will probably need a minimum of two months, but remember that every student is different.

Really think about your schedule. Will you be working full-time or part-time when you study for the LSAT? Will you have to take care of children? What other commitments must you attend to? Sit down and see how many months you are going to need in order to realistically achieve your target score on the LSAT.

Studying for the LSAT is an exponential climb. In the beginning, you will want to work slowly, really getting through each concept and new technique. After each lesson, set aside time to practice, so that each new strategy can really sink in and become second nature. Focus on reviewing everything you have learned at the end of each week.

Once you have learned all of the techniques and strategies, you will move into the second phase of LSAT prep. Start taking one full-length LSAT prep test (i.e., five full sections, including a 15-minute break and an experimental section) per week. If you find that you do not have the time to take one prep test every week, try taking individual timed sections instead of full exams some weeks. If you do this, sit through at least two back-to-back sections to build up your stamina.

If you are wondering how to take a five-section LSAT when LSAC does not release the experimental section, the answer is quite simple. Just plug another section from a different LSAT into the exam, and voilà! Keep in mind that while this section is technically "experimental," for the purpose of your LSAT prep, it is not. It is just another section from a previous LSAT, so it is another gauge of how you are doing. And since you will not know which section is experimental on your actual LSAT, it is a good idea to get used to treating all five sections as though they are scored.

For those of you who are still looking for a numerical answer to the "how much to study" question, let's start with the following as your baseline, which you can tailor to your specific needs. Try starting out with four to five hours of prep every day. If you like, give yourself one day off per week.

Remember, studying for the LSAT is an active process. Think about studying for the LSAT as an old-school, Blockbuster video store from the 1990s as opposed to Netflix streaming. Back in the day, if you wanted to rent a movie, you had to get off the couch, get into your car, drive down to Blockbuster, browse through the endless aisles, pick a movie, rent it, drive back home, watch it, rewind it, and then drive back to Blockbuster to return it. Studying for the LSAT is similar. You are going to have to put in the time and the effort. Sadly, there is no instant stream for mastering the LSAT.

All that being said, it is imperative that you do not burn yourself out during your prep and before your actual exam. Four hours of focused and energized studying is much more effective than six hours of lackluster and distracted studying. If you start to notice mental fatigue, there is no reason to proceed. Take a break, and come back to it later.

How Many Practice LSATs Should I Take?

Ideally, you want to take as many as possible. At the very minimum, try to take at least ten full-length digital LSATs.

The more practice LSATs you take, the better. As we noted above, if you do not have enough time to take all the practice LSATs you have as full-length exams in one sitting, you can break each practice exam into individual sections for timed practice. Most importantly, use only real LSAT questions.

LSATMax offers every single LSAT ever released by LSAC. You can also buy the real exams directly from LSAC on their website.

Should I Cancel My LSAT Score?

This used to be a much more difficult question to answer. As we have discussed, almost every law school used to average LSAT scores together. Therefore, if you felt like you did not do very well on an exam, it would be detrimental for you to keep your score. However, most law schools no longer average LSAT scores; instead, they take only the highest one. You need to research whether the school(s) in which you are interested average LSAT scores or instead consider only the highest score. This will be crucial in your decision to cancel or not.

We like to remind LSAT students that *you do not actually*

know how you did for certain. No matter what you think tripped you up, remember that the LSAT is graded on a curve. If there was a very odd question that threw you for a loop, chances are it did the same for most people.

Another reason to be wary of canceling is that LSAC will report the fact of the cancelation to law schools—and having lots of canceled scores doesn't look good. Therefore, you do not want to "just sit for the exam" if you are not ready.

There are, however, times you definitely should cancel. For example, Mehran canceled his first LSAT attempt because he made a mistake on a Logic Game that he thankfully caught, but did not have time to correct. He was fully aware that without a perfect score on Logic Games, he would not be able to reach his target score of 170+, so he canceled. This is a great example of why it is important to know your target score and how you plan to accomplish it (i.e., the number of questions you can miss per section).

Canceling is best considered on a case-by-case basis. The rule of thumb, however, is that you should not cancel, unless circumstances were highly out of the ordinary, or you were not properly prepared in the first place.

Bonus: What is LSAT-Flex?

In early 2020, the COVID-19 pandemic swept across the United States, and most in-person exams, including the March and April LSATs, were canceled. In May, LSAC rolled out the LSAT-Flex, which is a shorter exam that is taken remotely, usually from the exam taker's home.

As of this writing, LSAC continues to offer only LSAT-Flex exams. It seems likely that in-person exams will resume when it becomes safe to have them. What is not clear, however, is whether LSAC will continue to offer the LSAT-Flex as an alternative to in-person testing when that happens.

Taking an LSAT-Flex

The LSAT-Flex is intended to be taken at home, and it must be taken on a desktop or laptop computer, not a tablet (iPad), phone, or some other mobile device. Yes, that's different than the standard LSAT, which is taken on a tablet with a stylus, both of which are provided to students at the testing center.

The exam is administered through the ProctorU testing platform, and your performance will be monitored by a live proctor via your webcam and microphone. Video and audio will be recorded and subjected to further review after the exam, both by humans and with artificial intelligence (AI) techniques.

The rules

LSAC spends a lot of time worrying about people cheating on the LSAT, and the rules they have announced for the LSAT-Flex show that this situation is no different.

During the test, you may have with you only:

- Five blank sheets of scratch paper
- Valid ID

- No. 2 or HB pencils
- Highlighter
- Eraser (no mechanical erasers or erasers with sleeves)
- Pencil sharpener
- Tissues
- Beverage in a plastic container or juice box (max size of 20 oz/591 ml). No aluminum cans
- A non-digital wristwatch strapped to your wrist
- All other items must be put away

During the test, you may not:

- Communicate with anyone other than the proctor
- Read aloud
- Remove your face from the webcam's view
- Leave your seat
- Run prohibited software
- Access prohibited materials
- Connect or disconnect external storage devices
- Copy/save any test material or your written notes on your computer

All and only the same subject matter

The good news is that, as far as what is tested, nothing

has changed. Instead, the LSAT-Flex is just a shorter version of a standard LSAT.

The LSAT-Flex consists of three 35-minute sections:

- 1 Logical Reasoning
- 1 Reading Comprehension
- 1 Logic Games

For comparison, a standard LSAT consists of five 35-minute sections:

- 2 Logical Reasoning
- 1 Reading Comprehension
- 1 Logic Games
- 1 Experimental

Remember, the Experimental section is one extra section of Logical Reasoning, Reading Comp, or Logic Games that does not count toward your score. So, the LSAT-Flex is the same as a standard LSAT, just with no Experimental and one less Logical Reasoning section.

The biggest difference, therefore, is that Logical Reasoning is no longer the dominant section type. On the LSAT-Flex, each section counts for about 1/3 of your score. For that reason, studying for the LSAT-Flex might mean focusing a little less on Logical Reasoning and a little more on the other two sections, but that's it.

Given that it's shorter, there is one significant change you can make to your studying: taking more practice exams. Three sections of LSAT is far less draining than five, so take several practice exams a week, especially in the last few weeks before the exam. You can take any previous LSAT in LSAT-Flex form on the LSATMax website at lsatmax.com.

Scoring

The LSAT-Flex is scored in much the same way as a standard LSAT, which is to say that it's scored on a very complicated curve. The curve on a standard LSAT changes from exam to exam, but not by much.

So far, it looks like the LSAT-Flex curve follows that pattern. The percentage of questions you answer correctly on the LSAT-Flex should, in theory, get you the about the same score as if you got that percentage of questions correct on a full LSAT.

For example, on the June 2015 LSAT, a raw score of 83 out of 100 would get you a 165. Assuming that the LSAT-Flex has about 75 questions, a similar score of 83% would mean you'd need to get about 62 correct out of 75 to get a 165.

Score Preview

In connection with the LSAT-Flex, LSAC is offering first-time test takers to opportunity to learn their scores before canceling them. Up until now, exam takers wouldn't have received their scores by the time they cancel. This is available for $45 before the test, and $75 thereafter. Note that you'll have to complete the LSAT Writing Sample to be eligible.

Also, the $45 price ends at 11:59 pm Eastern time the day before the first day of testing for a particular exam administration. For example, testing might begin on a Saturday, even though your appointment to take the exam is on a Tuesday. If that's the case, you'd need to sign up by 11:59 pm Friday evening to get the lower price, even though your test wouldn't be for several more days.

What if I can't meet the computer and/or private room requirements?

A lot of people don't have a laptop or a desktop computer that meets the requirements for the LSAT-Flex. LSAC has helped a large number of students by loaning them laptops. And plenty of people don't have a living situation that allows them to shut everyone else out of a room for 3 hours. LSAC is working with those test takers to get them into hotel rooms or other accommodations at little or no cost.

If these or any other limitations make it hard for you to meet the requirements to take the LSAT-Flex, reach out to LSAC early about finding accommodations that will allow you to take the exam. To get accommodations, call the Candidate Services team at (215) 968-1001 or email LSACinfo@LSAC.org.

QUESTIONS YOU SHOULD ASK

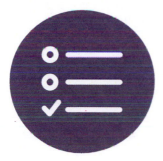

Are You Preparing With Real Questions?

Take a step back for a moment, and ask yourself: what is the purpose of the LSAT? What is the purpose of any standardized test, for that matter? The purpose of standardized testing is to measure certain skills so that applicants can be compared to each other during the admissions process.

The purpose of the LSAT is to measure your critical thinking skills and ability to analyze logically, in hopes of gauging how well you can implement this way of thinking—both during law school and beyond. Therefore, the most important factor in your LSAT prep course is not your instructor, class, or calendar, but whether or not you are preparing with real LSAT questions. Only by studying with real questions will you guarantee that by the end of your prep, you will be 100% familiar with the actual questions and concepts that you will encounter on the actual LSAT.

Made-up LSAT questions do not go through the rigorous process that LSAC uses to test every new LSAT question. What does this mean? Studying with made-up LSAT questions will be to your detriment. Remember, studying for standardized tests is all about conditioning. The more you study with real questions, the more familiar you will become with the actual exam. Repetition is key for improving your score. Improving your familiarity with the LSAT's format and questions is the best way to hone your skills and get the score you want. Therefore, using real questions is the best way to maximize your score.

Remember, the LSAC offers real, licensed questions for purchase. Therefore, the real questions are available to all LSAT prep courses to license and offer to their students. Again, LSAC now publishes a list of official licensees so you should definitely confirm that the course you are considering appears on this list. An important question to ask, considering that the real questions are available via license, is: why would a course not offer them? LSATMax uses only real LSAT questions and we offer every real, officially-licensed LSAT that LSAC has made available. Prep Tests are also available directly through LSAC. Any student can purchase these Prep Tests, but if you are thinking about purchasing an LSAT prep course, make sure you also pick one that includes all of these exams.

Is Law School For Me?

Let's take a step back and consider the big picture. Why are you taking the LSAT? To go to law school. Why do you want to go to law school? It consists of three very difficult years, filled with gunner students who will cause you to reevaluate your own intelligence and academic self-worth; professors who make you want to rip your hair out with the amount of reading they assign; and memos that go on and on, but never end up being quite good enough. There is also the debt that will accumulate year after year and will eventually amount to a six-figured monster chained to your heels. Sounds lovely, right?

There needs to be a reason you want to face all of this

turmoil, and that reason needs to be good. Maybe being a lawyer has always been a dream of yours. If that is the case, really make sure you know what it means to be a lawyer. Talk to many different types of lawyers, and ask them what they do on a daily basis. What are their tasks? What are their weekly, monthly, and yearly goals? Really try to understand what you are getting yourself into.

We have compiled a list of common "reasons" for going to law school that we hear from our own students, and explanations showing why these reasons should not determine that law school is for you.

Everyone says I'm good at arguing.

Very few lawyers ever partake in anything similar to the conventional "argument." Most people who say they like to argue tend to argue more to be contentious than for the intellectual challenge of it. Furthermore, with the exception of the top law schools, you will not find yourself stuck in intellectual discourse during your studies or lectures. You will learn black-letter law, and if you are lucky, you might get thrown a question asking how you *feel* about the consequences of such laws.

I have always loved Suits (or some other legal TV show or movie).

No television show has ever correctly depicted life as a lawyer (except maybe *Better Call Saul*—just kidding!). If you do not know that by now, you need a huge reality check. The practice of law is not this romantic, drama-filled career where you get to yell, "I want the truth!" and give five-minute speeches before every witness interrogation. Being a lawyer is tedious and, quite frankly, boring. TV writers would never want to create a show about some lawyer writing out interrogatories and serving them in a timely manner.

I want to save the world.

Though becoming an attorney can put you on a path toward bettering the world, you need to make sure you know what you are getting yourself into. Most "change the world" jobs do not pay much, and you may find yourself forced to get a high-paying corporate job to pay off your law school loans—all the more reason to be patient during your LSAT prep and truly maximize your LSAT score. The higher your score, the more financial aid you will be offered. If going to law school in order to help people is really your dream, there are loan forgiveness programs geared toward public service jobs. At the federal level, the Public Service Loan Forgiveness Program (PSLF) is intended to encourage individuals to enter and continue to work full-time in public service jobs. Under this program, borrowers may qualify for forgiveness of the remaining balance of their Direct Loans after they have made 120 qualifying payments (i.e., ten years) while employed full-time by certain public service employers.

Some law schools have similar programs. For instance, Harvard Law School has a program called the Low Income Protection Plan (LIPP). LIPP was the first law school program to address the inability of law students with massive educational debt to pursue careers in public service, which are traditionally low-paying jobs. By repaying these students' debts, LIPP allows HLS graduates to pursue their true passions without worrying about how they are going to repay their law school loans.

If you want to go to law school because you want to make positive contributions to the world around you, be sure you educate yourself about debt management strategies and repayment assistance programs, so that you can actually do the work you want to do after you have graduated.

I don't have anything else to do.

This is the worst possible reason to go to law school. If you do not know what to do, then why would you want to choose a ridiculously rigorous, three-year course load that will leave you with hundreds of thousands of dollars of debt just to find out that you may not actually like being a lawyer? It is okay if you do not know what you want to do. Take the time to really think about it. Do some research, ask people, and get your hands dirty!

This reason actually comes up a lot with humanities majors. They ask themselves, "Well, what else am I going to do with my undergraduate degree?" But law school should never be a "*shrug* I-haven't-got-anything-better-to-do" option.

I want to be *rich*.

People look at corporate attorneys and think, *$160,000 a year is bomb!* Let's take a moment and put this into perspective. First, the number of high-paying corporate law jobs is extremely limited (and artificial intelligence could further exacerbate this issue very quickly). Many law school graduates find themselves saddled with a debt load that presumes a six-figure salary—but they cannot land a job that pays such a salary. Second, most large corporate firms that pay this kind of dough require somewhere between 1,900-2,000 annual billable hours from their associates. This represents the total number of hours of *actual* work you can bill directly to a client. On average, it takes about ten hours in the office to accrue seven billable hours. This means a typical attorney has to work about 2,700 real hours per year to meet their minimum "billables." They are working 7.5 hours EVERY SINGLE DAY OF THE YEAR.

If you divide the salary by the number of hours, you get $50 per hour. There are myriad jobs that pay this amount (or more!) and do not require three years of law school (much less the stress of corporate firm life): funeral director, marketing manager, financial aid officer, LSAT prep instructor, etc. Don't get us wrong—being an attorney is one way to possibly make a lot of money, but it is certainly not a guaranteed way, nor is it the only way.

Make no mistake: we do not want to discourage you from pursuing your law school dreams. We just want to forewarn you to be diligent in your research of what law school and being an attorney actually entails. Some really great people to talk to are your parents, undergraduate pre-law advisers, professional admissions counselors, actual lawyers, and law students.

Your college prelaw adviser can also act as a great, impartial resource in helping you decide if law school and you are a match made in heaven. You should also make sure to talk to real lawyers who are practicing what you would like to practice, as well as law students attending the law schools you are considering.

Having a hard time finding knowledgeable people to talk with about law school? You can always reach out to us via chat, email or by calling 855.483.7862 Monday-Friday 9am-6pm PT. You can also text "LSAT" to 310-818-7743 to schedule a free consult with us.

What Happens If I Don't Get The Score I Want?

Don't let your LSAT score bring you down. If you didn't score in the range you were hoping for, you can take the exam again! As we have discussed, it used to be the norm for law schools to average your various LSAT scores. Now, however, it is more common for law schools to take your highest LSAT score. With that said, make sure to double-check with each school you are applying to. As mentioned earlier, the rule of thumb is to abstain from taking the LSAT until you are ready. There is no harm in postponing an exam!

Remember that the material on the LSAT is all based upon patterns and a specific way of thinking. The LSAT is a test of endurance, not knowledge. Your greatest tools are simple strategy and relentless practice.

LSATMax hands you both of these tools. First, learn the strategies via a comprehensive LSAT prep course. Second, practice, practice, practice on as many real LSATs as possible. Every student is different. You might need X amount of hours on one section, with only Y in another. Once you have the strategies down, practicing under time pressure is the key.

With the number of law school applications still down (although rebounding at the moment; "The Trump Bump" according to some), now is a great time to score high on the LSAT and apply to law school. Remember, the LSAT is not hard; it is just hard work. If you want to retake your exam, make sure to buckle down and prepare. Schedule your next few months of prep, and decide which materials you would like to use.

If you are going to sign up for an LSAT prep course, make sure you consider the duration of your access to course materials. This is a really important factor when deciding which LSAT prep course to purchase. Most LSAT prep courses cut off your access to the materials after 10-12 weeks. They do not take into consideration the possibility that you might not be fully prepared and therefore want to study longer, or that you may be unhappy with the score you received and wish to continue studying.

With LSATMax, time is one your side. LSATMax offers every student lifetime access to all course materials. LSATMax students never have to worry about losing access to materials they have already paid for. We do this because we realize that the vast majority of LSAT-takers will not reach their peak within 10 to 12 weeks. An LSAT prep course is only step one of the process. You must leave ample time to practice and hone these skills. A recent study by LSAC confirmed this fact when it revealed that mean LSAT scores were highest for second-time takers.

Finally, consider the GRE instead. A couple of years ago, certain law schools began accepting the GRE in addition to the LSAT for admissions. Some students prefer the GRE, which is a subject-based exam (unlike the LSAT) that is offered much more frequently than the LSAT and which can be used to apply to non-law graduate programs as well.

Research the law schools to which you wish to apply. If they accept the GRE, consider whether that test is a better fit for you than the LSAT. And just in case, you didn't know, there's an app for that as well—**GREMax GRE Prep!**

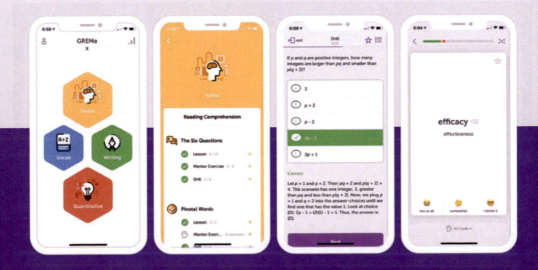

Available in These App Stores

How Can I Mentally And Physically Prepare For The LSAT?

The main factor in physically and emotionally preparing for the LSAT is taking care of yourself. You know the drill: drink water, sleep, eat healthy (making sure not to skip breakfast), exercise, and relax!

Let's get into some of the specifics. What is one of the biggest factors that can negatively affect your LSAT prep? Fatigue. Namely, brain fatigue: the state of having low mental energy, and being easily distracted, forgetful, and mentally flighty. Every student preparing for the LSAT will experience brain fatigue. You are only human, and your ability to stay focused has its limits. How many times have you been in a situation where you finished reading a question and realized you have no idea what you just read? Many? That means you are suffering from brain fatigue.

Luckily, one of the best ways to rid yourself of this ailment is to take a break. Go out for a walk: studies have shown that natural settings, such as a park or a beach, are calming. In such settings, your brain can rest and reset its overused resources to help reduce your mental fatigue. People who live near trees and parks have lower levels of cortisol, a stress hormone, in their saliva than those who live amid concrete and buildings. Does this mean you should move? Possibly, but not based on this— we know better than to mistake correlation for causation!

Nevertheless, it is really important to take the time to relax once in a while. Take a break from your LSAT prep, and let your mind rest. Think about it: when you work out, if you keep working on the same muscle, it will never grow. You need to work out and then rest, giving your muscles time to recuperate. Your brain is the same. We are not saying take a week off; just try to set aside a few leisure hours during the day to read, watch a TV show, take a walk in a park or garden, or whatever else makes you smile.

Sleep is also crucial. Study after study shows that getting enough sleep—around seven to eight hours a night—is essential for optimal brain function. It seems intuitive, but so many students deprive themselves of sleep just so they can get a few more hours of LSAT prep in each day. This is counterproductive.

At some point, many LSAT prep students may want to sleep, but they feel too anxious to actually get some shut-eye. We have compiled a list of things you can do to try to optimize your ability to rest.

1. Get rid of all those distractions.

Turn off your iPhones, iPads, televisions, and laptops—basically anything that is constantly tempting you to waste your precious sleep time. How often have you finished studying and, instead of getting to bed at a decent hour, turned on Netflix or HBO and started watching an entire season of *Breaking Bad*? Devices such as the Kindle are not too bad as long as they are not backlit, because they are roughly equivalent to reading a book. The backlighting on devices is troublesome, because it tricks your brain into thinking it should stay awake (because it is being exposed to light). If you really just cannot leave these devices in your living room, at the very least, stop using them 30 minutes before your target bedtime. Without adequate sleep, your brain functioning will be decreased, which will make it more difficult to make good decisions quickly—something crucial to your success on the LSAT.

2. Be physically active during the day.

Being physically active helps your body tire itself out, so when it is finally time for bed, it is much easier to fall asleep. Exercise also increases blood flow to the brain, keeping it healthy. This is important when you are preparing to take a stressful and strenuous exam. Developing a habit of physical exercise early on in your adult life will also help you in manifold ways. Regular exercise now can help you continue regular exercise in law school and beyond (and help you survive the stresses of law school exams, the bar exam, and the practice of law).

3. Keep your mind calm and clear of stress.

There are methods that can assist you in keeping a clear head. For instance, meditating before you start the day and before you go to bed can help you stay calm and less stressed. Even just five minutes of time spent focusing on your breathing and trying to calm your "thinking brain" can have enormous benefits for your psyche, energy levels, and overall attitude.

Practice using affirmations. Studies have shown that affirmations strengthen your confidence and drive. During your affirmation, visualize yourself opening your LSAT score, and seeing your target score. Write the following down on a piece of paper every morning and evening before you meditate:

> *It feels so gratifying to have achieved the score I wanted on the LSAT. All those months of hard work have now come to fruition.*

Then, on to your meditation! Meditation is your path to a quiet, healthy, calm mind. We encourage you to meditate once in the morning and once at night. Set aside three minutes of your morning for meditation. Make your bed and sit on it. Stay quiet, and pay attention to your body and mind through your breath. Encourage your mind to stop spinning and churning during those three minutes. This is great practice to help still your mind for better performance on the exam (and in life).

By performing these exercises to quell your fears and/or visualizing your ability to succeed on the LSAT, you will actually have more restful sleep.

Just try it. There is no harm in being less distracted, exercising, and meditating. If it does not help you on the LSAT, it will at least help you create a healthy and fit lifestyle.

4. Stay Hydrated.

The next big thing is staying hydrated. Water is your best friend while you study. Water is a natural remedy for headaches. Drinking more water will also make you less prone to getting sick. Try to drink at least eight glasses of water a day. Staying hydrated improves your immune system, which helps keep you as vibrant and healthy as possible.

Water also relieves fatigue. It acts as your natural energy drink. Your body uses water to flush out toxins and waste products. These toxins weigh you down mentally and physically. If the toxins stay in your body, you will be more sluggish and less alert. If your body lacks water, it has to work harder to function. For instance, the heart has to work harder to pump oxygenated blood to your cells. Without adequate hydration, your heart and the rest of your vital organs will be exhausted, and so will you.

Drinking more water can make the difference between walking into your test center healthy and alert, or fatigued and with the "sniffles." Along with keeping a hydrated body, you need to keep a well-nourished body. Eating well every day will allow your mind to stay strong, energized, and efficient.

5. Find Balance.

Lastly, make sure you continue to have a social life. Many students tend to isolate themselves from their friends and family when preparing for the LSAT (and again in law school). While it is important to cut down on your social life to prioritize the attainment of your goals, completely depriving yourself of any time off with family and friends will not help you stay happy and healthy. Help yourself stay sane, happy, and productive by keeping a balance between your social life and your LSAT-prep life.

That being said, we would highly recommend giving up drinking, along with any other recreational activities that can have a detrimental impact on your mental focus. This does not have to be a permanent life change, but it is a great decision during your LSAT prep.

When Should I Take The LSAT?

Until recently, the LSAT was administered four times each year. Between June 2019 and April 2020, however, the exam will be administered nine times (June 2019, July 2019, September 2019, October 2019, November 2019, January 2020, February 2020, March 2020, and April 2020). Although there is no definitive answer for which test administration is the "best" option, your personal law school application timeline can affect which exam is best for you.

First, you need to decide whether or not you want to

take a year or more off before law school, or if you would like to go straight out of undergrad. If you do not want to take time off, the best time to take the LSAT is the summer between your junior and senior year of college. Many students, however, choose to take the LSAT in the fall, which gives them an entire summer to study unhindered by the responsibility of studying for other courses or working. The rule of thumb is the earlier the better, since you will have more time in case you want to retake the test but still have your score considered by admissions committees for the following admissions year.

The earlier you apply to schools, the better your chances, because law school admissions officers look at the applications in the order they trickle in. Every law school uses a "rolling admissions" system; therefore, the earlier you send in your application, the sooner the admissions officers will look at your application packet. If you apply early, you will be compared to fewer people at a time when more seats are available. The longer you wait, the more you will have to compete against a greater number of applicants for a smaller number of available seats.

Even when considering rolling admissions, if you are choosing between applying early with a low LSAT score and applying later with a higher LSAT score, always choose the latter. Remember, your LSAT score is 75-80%

of your application!

Who Is My Instructor?

This is a really important question that students rarely ask. It is crucial to research and learn as much as possible about your LSAT instructor. How long have they been teaching the LSAT? Did they actually prepare for the LSAT, or have they merely taken an LSAT training course? What did the instructor score on the LSAT? Did they score above a 172 (99th percentile), and if so, how long did it take them to get there? Do they know what it is like to have to raise their score significantly, or did the LSAT just come naturally to them? Have they taken an actual LSAC-proctored LSAT, or have they only ever taken practice LSATs proctored by their supervisors?

Your instructor will be your guide during the next few months of your LSAT prep. He or she is the Jedi Knight to your Padawan. The Qui-Gon Jinn to your Obi-Wan. The Obi-Wan to your Anakin Skywalker. The . . . you get the idea. Why would you not want to know their credentials?

For example, some well-known LSAT prep companies do not even require their instructors to have scored in the 99th percentile. This means that these instructors will be trying to teach you something they were never able to accomplish themselves. Avoid these instructors like the plague.

How long your instructor has been teaching the LSAT is also very important, especially when considering the extremely high turnover rate in LSAT prep instructors (i.e., most LSAT prep instructors eventually go on to become lawyers, and never look back). Doing well on the LSAT does not necessarily mean that you can teach others how to do well. After teaching a few dozen classes, an instructor will slowly hone their techniques and teaching skills to attain instructor perfection.

Moreover, if your instructor was a natural and did not have to study very hard for the exam, they will not know what it feels like to struggle and hit walls with an LSAT score. They will not know firsthand what it is like to run out of time or constantly pick the wrong answer after eliminating all but two. These are important questions to ask.

LSATMax instructors have years of LSAT prep experience. Moreover, they each started with a lower score before studying their way to the 99th percentile on a real, LSAC-proctored LSAT. And since LSATMax is an on-demand LSAT prep course, we have eliminated the variation in the quality of instruction found in traditional, in-class LSAT prep courses.

Which Test Center Should I Choose?

Contrary to popular belief, every LSAT location is not the same. Obviously, it is important to try to get a location that is very close to you, and avoid a location on a route with heavy traffic congestion. Given that the popular locations fill up rather quickly, it is also important to lock down your LSAT location as soon as possible. Let's discuss your options.

The best places are universities in your area. Why? Because a university gives you an unconscious study vibe, and often you can actually go to the university and study

in the rooms where the test will be administered. As
we have discussed before, mimicking testing conditions
during your LSAT prep is imperative. Being able to take
practice exams in the actual room, or at least in a similar
room, can be quite helpful. If your test is in the morning,
you'll need to get your mind accustomed to being fully
alert and awake by 8:00 a.m.—ready for four hours of
intense concentration and focus. You want to be as
exact as possible. If your exam is on a Saturday, get your
mind and body ready for Saturday morning exams. Train
your mind to equate Saturday mornings with logic and
concentration; the same goes for afternoon and Monday
LSATs.

Each school is different, however, so additional research
may be warranted. What kinds of desks are available to
test takers? Is there a lot of ambient noise around the
test site (e.g., construction noise)? Is parking a hassle?
Whatever state you live in, ask your friends and other
people you know who have already taken the exam what
they thought of their testing center to help gauge where
the best place in your state is located.

Try to get yourself accustomed to the environment. If
you choose a school as your testing location, you will
most likely be able to go to campus each morning and
take a practice LSAT at your testing center. It is true that

you may not be able to find your exact classroom (or even building), but getting acquainted with being in the general testing location will help calm your test-day nerves.

Every little thing counts. If you get to the testing location and find that a specific sound on Saturday mornings bothers you, then you can reschedule or relocate your LSAT, or work through the sound by practicing in that spot. You will become well-acquainted with how the air conditioning works or does not work. You will know where the bathrooms and the vending machines are. Do you see what we are saying? Also, driving to the testing location every Saturday morning—again assuming that you are taking the exam on a Saturday morning as opposed to in the afternoon or on a Monday—will get you acclimated to the normal traffic and routes near the location.

What if the logic gods are not smiling on you the morning of your exam and decide to cause a HUGE accident on whatever freeway you have to take? Well, since you, our smart and well-prepared LSAT-takers, are well-acquainted with that area, you will be able to find alternate routes, and plan accordingly for traffic. If you are not well-acquainted with the route, then download the *Waze* app, and cross your fingers.

Another benefit of choosing a university or college as your testing center is that while you take your actual exam, the environment will be filled mostly with educators and students who understand that it is important to stay quiet near a testing location. It is more likely that these passersby will respect the situation and keep the environment as quiet as they can for you.

Sometimes, however, universities can be horrible environments for test-taking, depending upon what is happening on campus that day. For instance, we know of an LSAT nightmare that occurred during a December LSAT on USC's campus. There was a football game at noon that day, which meant that the USC marching band was parading around campus in preparation for the game, rousing not only the Trojan fans, but also the poor LSAT-takers. Be aware of what is going on the day of your exam. It could make or break the location for you.

Locations you need to stay away from include the various hotels and motels where the test is offered. We have heard horror stories of the testing rooms at these locations being very close to the lobby, or not having actual doors to keep noise out. The proctors administering the test have no interest in your score, let alone making sure that you have the best testing experience. The closer you can be to an educational environment, the more likely it is that the proctors will take the whole experience seriously. Patrons at a hotel or motel really do not care about you and your nonexistent social life for the past few months. Do not let a random family visiting Disneyland for the first time kill your Reading Comprehension section.

So, what must you do? Find the list of the testing locations closest to you. If your campus is a testing location, CHOOSE THAT ONE! Do not leave this to the last minute, when you will have no choice but to take your LSAT at the Best Western . . . which will also be hosting little Susie so-and-so's pre-Disneyland sleepover.

What Can I Do Outside of My LSAT Prep That Will Help My LSAT Score?

First and foremost, the best thing to do outside of your LSAT prep is to relax and take care of yourself. Since we have already gone over this, let's discuss a neat trick you can do outside of your LSAT prep that will actually help raise your score.

Let's talk Reading Comprehension. The passages are taken from actual scientific, legal, and literary journals, and tweaked to work for the LSAT. What does this mean? Well, not only are you actually learning real facts and theories that you can then regurgitate at your next social gathering (where all the guests can *ooh* and *ahh* at how worldly you are for knowing the ritualistic patterns of African mask art or Freud's interpretation of Hansel and Gretel as an allegory describing the state of our children's psyches), but you can also hone your LSAT Reading Comprehension skills by subscribing to well-written periodicals.

At LSATMax, we have found that the more you read in your free time (what little you may have), the better your performance on the Reading Comprehension section of the exam—and Logical Reasoning, for that matter! Try to focus specifically upon denser, more academic material. Get a subscription to a scientific journal or academic review. Try reading a couple of articles a day during your downtime, and really focus on understanding the material you have read.

To this end, LSATMax Premium offers its students a 12-week digital subscription to *The Economist*. Getting your mind used to reading, understanding, and analyzing dense, not-so-action-packed reading material is a great way to improve your endurance and score on the Reading Comprehension passages.

Are There Any Benefits to an In-Class Prep Course?

If it is harder for you to motivate yourself to stick to a schedule or study on your own, you may feel that being in an "in-class" LSAT prep course could benefit you, as it gives you a sense of feigned accountability to attend class—and, possibly, some accountability to your instructor.

However, it is important to remember that your in-class course alone is not sufficient for optimizing your LSAT score. Studying for the LSAT requires a great deal of self-motivation and perseverance to begin with. No matter how you are studying, whether in class or through self-study, you need to have the discipline to sit down and practice for many hours every day.

Although an in-class course may create a faux-accountability that will get you to class, you still need to motivate yourself to practice outside of class. Remember the Blockbuster video analogy! Your course is only step one of the process. Step two is practice, practice, practice.

Another very important thing to consider before choosing an in-class course is the limited access. Every in-class LSAT prep course on the market will limit your access (generally 10 to 12 weeks), and will charge you again if you want to continue to prepare. We have already discussed the wide range of quality offered by in-class LSAT prep instructors, but you should also be aware that, by definition, every in-class LSAT prep course teaches to the mean. This will cause some students to feel held back, while other students will feel left behind.

For all of these reasons, we feel that on-demand LSAT prep courses are a superior option. Because of the low overhead, self-study options are generally more affordable than in-class ones. A self-study course also revolves around your schedule, so you'll never have to worry about missing class due to life's unexpected surprises.

Moreover, if your self-study course does not require an Internet connection, as is the case with LSATMax, you can literally study from anywhere. Access to "pause" and "rewind" buttons for every lecture also means that you will never have the feeling of being held back or left behind by the pace of the lessons.

We truly believe that the only benefit of an in-class LSAT prep course is the ability to ask your instructor questions; and, for this reason, we have created real-time chat and message boards that allow our students to ask us questions 24/7. While LSATMax is a remote learning process, our students are not alone.

LSATMax has taken the idea of customized LSAT prep even one step further by introducing detailed analytics that will track your progress and highlight your strengths and weaknesses as you progress through the course. This data will transform LSATMax into your personal, portable, on-demand private LSAT tutor.

Why Is My LSAT Prep Course So Expensive?

This is a really important question that all prospective LSAT students should ask themselves. Remember what you have read in this book. You can buy every available real LSAT from LSAC for a couple hundred dollars online.

Let's pretend, for a moment, that the LSAT course you are considering uses only real questions. Where does the other $1000+ in price come in? One could argue that it is a combination of the 10 to 12 weeks of lectures, plus the attention you get from your in-class instructor; but hopefully, this book has given you some perspective.

We have discussed the various perils you should be aware of with in-class LSAT instructors: being underqualified and/or inexperienced, or having to teach to the mean of the class, which often leaves students feeling like they have no other option than to pay extra for private tutoring.

Access is another issue we have discussed. Once this expensive course is done, students are forced to pay again if they would like to have continued access to their materials. So does the $1000+ for an LSAT prep course still make sense? Does this exorbitant price tag seem worth it?

As you know, LSATMax only uses real LSAT questions, offering every single one available to its students along with lifetime access to instructors, lectures, and materials. LSATMax instructors are second to none. LSATMax's strategies are proven and easy to use. Students have 24/7 access to our instructors via on-demand videos and our live message-board community. Since our app does not require an Internet connection, students can literally study anywhere they want, anytime.

Not only is our course the most affordable on the market, it is also the only LSAT prep course that includes lifetime access and support. Students never have to worry about losing access to the materials they have already paid for. Even at this lower price point, LSATMax offers its students exponentially more than our competitors. This is the beauty of technology.

Lastly, as the pioneer of mobile LSAT prep and the first company to put a digital LSAT on a tablet, no LSAT company can match LSATMax's experience in the digital LSAT era. In fact, you can simulate the digital LSAT experience right now by downloading our free app on an iPad or Android tablet and tapping on the "free LSAT" icon.

It is time to ask yourself: why is my LSAT prep course so ridiculously expensive?

It's something to think about!

IN CONCLUSION . . .

We hope this book has helped to put at least a slight dent in the myriad questions you may have about the LSAT and your LSAT prep. We cannot promise you that it is going to be easy, but we can promise that if you work hard, it will pay off in the end.

The best plan is to do your homework on the different LSAT prep courses available. Look at your own study strengths and weaknesses, and choose an LSAT prep course that you believe will best optimize your chances of getting the LSAT score you want. This, in turn, will help you gain admission to the law school of your dreams.

We appreciate the time you have spent reading this. Remember, LSATMax is here for you. If you haven't already, make sure to download our free app from the Apple App Store and/or Google Play Store.

You can also sign up for a free LSATMax account at:
https://testmaxprep.com/lsat/signup

In addition to daily drills and a real practice digital
LSAT complete with detailed score report, analytics and
explanations, you can actually get started with our back-
to-back-to-back #1-rated LSAT prep course.

Nothing to lose, everything to gain . . .

If you have any questions, please feel free to contact us at
any time. You can email us at **support@testmaxprep.com**
or text "LSAT" to 310-818-7743 to schedule a free consult
with our LSAT prep experts.

Wishing you all the best,
The **lsatmax** Team

Try The #1-Rated LSAT Prep for Free.

Get 10% Off When You Enroll.

Kyle Ryman
Texas A&M

I scored below a 150 on my first practice LSAT in November. **In June I took the LSAT and scored a 170. I couldn't have done it without LSATMax.**

Anita Yandle
University of Washington

The tutorials from LSATMax helped me get my 99th percentile score! It was great to have the videos at my fingertips at all times so that I could study any time I had a moment.

Austin Sheehy
University of Central Oklahoma

LSATMax is my hero! **My starting score was around a 155-158, and I scored a 170 on the June LSAT!**

Naader Banki
USC

I used LSATMax to study for the October LSAT. **I started out with a diagnostic somewhere in the 150s, and improved my score to 166 on the October test.**

To Redeem Visit lsatmax.io/180 or Call (855) 294-4553

Claim Your Free 30-Min LSAT Consultation

Ensure a strong start to your LSAT prep. Schedule your free LSAT consultation with a *99th percentile instructor*.

Visit lsatmax.io/consultation or Call (855) 294-4553